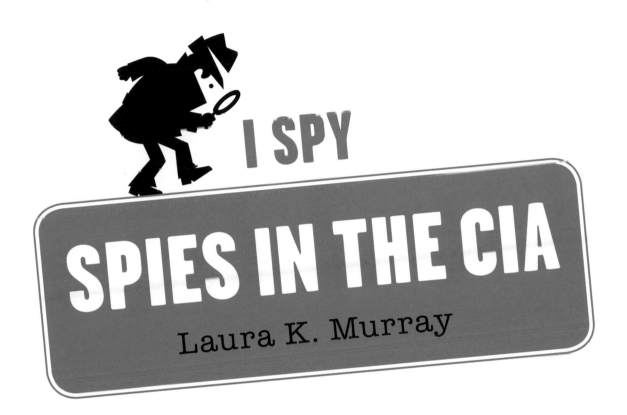

I SPY

SPIES IN THE CIA

Laura K. Murray

Creative Education ◉ Creative Paperbacks

Published by Creative Education and Creative Paperbacks
P.O. Box 227, Mankato, Minnesota 56002
Creative Education and Creative Paperbacks
are imprints of **The Creative Company**
www.thecreativecompany.us

Design and production by **Christine Vanderbeek**
Art direction by **Rita Marshall**
Printed in the **United States of America**

Photographs by Corbis (Ed Darack/Science Faction,
INA FASSBENDER/Reuters, Hulton-Deutsch Collection,
Jon Feingersh Photography/SuperStock, NASA/Science
Photo Library, Reuters, Alex Milan Tracy/Demotix,
Viaframe), Getty Images (Louis S. Glanzman/contributor),
Shutterstock (Alexandr III, BeRad, Milos Djapovic, M.
Luevanos, SoRad, tele52)

Library of Congress Cataloging-in-Publication Data
Murray, Laura K.
Spies in the CIA / Laura K. Murray.
p. cm. — (I spy)
Includes index.
Summary: An early reader's guide to CIA spies, introducing
American espionage history, famous agents such as Aldrich
Ames, technology such as spy satellites, and the dangers all
spies face.

ISBN 978-1-60818-616-7 (hardcover)
ISBN 978-1-62832-228-6 (pbk)
ISBN 978-1-56660-663-9 (eBook)
1. Intelligence—United States—Juvenile literature. 2.
Espionage, American—Juvenile literature. 3. Spies—
United States—Juvenile literature. 4. United States.
Central Intelligence Agency—Juvenile literature. I. Title.

JK468.I6M86 2015
327.1273—dc23   2014048718

CCSS: RI.1.1, 2, 3, 4, 5, 6, 7, 10; RI.2.1, 2, 3, 5, 6, 7; RI.3.1,
3, 5, 7; RF.1.1, 3, 4; RF.2.4

First Edition HC 9 8 7 6 5 4 3 2 1
First Edition PBK 9 8 7 6 5 4 3 2 1

TABLE OF CONTENTS

I SPY

AN AMERICAN SPY

Spies often have to
sneak into places.

IT IS NIGHT. AN AMERICAN

secret agent takes a deep
breath. She jumps from the
plane! She opens her chute.
Then she floats to the ground.
She does not want to get caught!

THE CIA

MADE IN
BOSTON
U.S.

PATENTED
NO 2082505
NO 2168941

Spy cameras may be
hidden inside books.

United States

SPIES WORK ALL OVER THE

world. They work in secret to
gather information. In the United
States, some spies work for the
CIA. This group began in 1947.

THE U.S. HAS HAD SPIES FOR

a long time. George Washington used spies in the 1700s. Spies like Mary Bowser worked during the **Civil War**.

A HISTORY OF SPYING

People on the ground
fly drone aircraft.

SPY SCHOOL

CIA SPIES NEED TO PASS

special tests. They study
weapons, airplanes, and
computers. Some spies speak
other languages, too.

The CIA makes special objects for spying.

THE CIA HAS SCHOOLS FOR

training spies. "The Farm" is in Virginia. "The Point" is in North Carolina. Spies learn how to read maps and drive backwards!

ALDRICH AMES WORKED

for the CIA. But he became a **mole** for Russia. He was arrested in 1994.

14

TOOLS OF THE TRADE

AMERICAN SPIES USE

disappearing ink and tiny cameras. Some cameras have wings. They fly around like bugs! Spy satellites take pictures from high above Earth.

Powers took secret
pictures from his plane.

SECRET AGENTS MUST BE

ready for anything. In 1960,
the Russians shot down a U.S.
spy plane. They put pilot
Francis Gary Powers in jail.

AMERICAN SPIES DO NOT

work alone. They get other people to tell secrets. Agents carry out their orders. Then they get ready for the next job!

NEVER DONE

TOP-SECRET ACTIVITY
#0961: Make Disappearing Ink

Spies use science and smart thinking to share secrets. Write a hidden message for a fellow spy!

Tools:
1/4 cup baking soda
1/4 cup water
Q-tip or thin
  paintbrush
paper
grape juice
  concentrate

Orders: In a small bowl, mix the baking soda and water. Dip a Q-tip or paintbrush into the mixture, and then write a secret message on a piece of paper. Let it dry. Lightly paint grape juice concentrate over the page. Watch as your message reappears!

Can you think of other ways to send a secret message?

GLOSSARY

agent   someone who works as a spy

chute   a big sheet that helps a person slow down after jumping from an airplane

Civil War   the American war between the Union (North) and Confederacy (South) that lasted from 1861 to 1865

mole   a spy who gives a group's secrets to an enemy

pilot   the person who flies an airplane

satellites   objects in space that move around Earth

READ MORE

David, Jack. *U-2 Planes.*
Minneapolis: Bellwether Media,
2008.

Stewart, James. *Spies and Traitors.*
North Mankato, Minn.: Smart Apple
Media, 2008.

WEBSITES

CIA: KIDS' ZONE
https://www.cia.gov/kids-page/games
Test your spy skills with puzzles and
games, and find pages to color.

INTERNATIONAL SPY MUSEUM: KIDSPY ZONE
*http://www.spymuseum.org
/education-programs/kids
-families/kidspy-zone/*
Play spy games, and learn how
to talk like a secret agent.

Note: Every effort has been made to ensure that the websites
listed above are suitable for children, that they have educational
value, and that they contain no inappropriate material. However,
because of the nature of the Internet, it is impossible to guaran-
tee that these sites will remain active indefinitely or that their
contents will not be altered.

INDEX